The Skipping Rope

Story by Jenny Giles
Illustrations by Sharyn Madder

Abby always liked going to play with her friend Clare.
Clare lived on a farm.

"What can we do today?" said Abby.

"Let's skip!" said Clare.
"I can get two ropes from the shed."

"But I can't skip," said Abby.

"Make the rope go over your head, like this," said Clare. "Then jump!"

Abby tried, but she tripped over. She looked at Clare, who was skipping very fast.

"I can't do that," said Abby.

"I had to try lots of times," said Clare, "and then, one day, I did it."

Abby tried again and again, but she still tripped over the rope.

Abby turned the rope one more time. She let it stay on the ground, and then she jumped over it.

"That's better!" said Clare.

"But I'm still not very good at it," said Abby. "I want to skip like you."

"The rope is too long for you," said Clare.
"I have a better one in my toy box. Let's go and get it."

Abby looked at the rope.
"**That** is a good one!" she said.
"Thanks, Clare."

Abby ran outside with the rope.

She made it go over her head.

Then she jumped

as it came down to her feet.

And this time, she did **not** trip!

Abby turned the rope round and round.
She jumped over it without tripping at all.

"I can do it!" she shouted.

"Look, Clare!" laughed Abby.

"I can skip like you now!"